Being Armed

Greg Reeser

ISBN: 978-0-578-68041-5

Printed in the United States of America
by Diggy Pod

First Printing edition 2020

Publisher: Greg Reeser
            gregreeser@charter.net

Cover design by Greg Reeser

To all freedom loving Americans who believe in their
God given right to defend themselves

Contents

Being Armed

Owning a gun and being armed are not the same thing. To be armed, your gun must be in your immediate possession and you must know the necessary steps to make it ready to fire. For example, if you have a loaded revolver, it is by definition ready to fire. If you have a semi-automatic pistol, it is not ready to fire until there is a round in the chamber. You must "rack" the slide in order to chamber a round. Additionally, if your loaded gun has a safety, and it is in the safe position, you must disengage the safety to make it ready to fire.

What do I mean by having your gun in your immediate possession? Put simply, your gun must be either on your person (preferably in a holster), in your hand, in a purse, fanny pack, carry case that you are holding, or even lying next to you where it is immediately accessible.

So, are you armed if you have your gun on your nightstand in the bedroom, but you are in your kitchen having a snack when two home invaders kick open your door? Obviously not, but this is exactly how 80% of defenders managed to fight off a home invasion by retrieving their gun from a place of storage*. Certainly the home defender would have a better chance of success if the gun were more accessible, but not everyone wants to wear their gun while at home.

Home invasion is the first thing about self-defense on the minds of concerned people these days, and rightfully so, as there is nothing more terrifying than the thought of some crazed maniac breaking into your home while you are asleep, or to be surprised while at a low alert level. It is critically important that you understand that the police cannot protect you at a time like this. There is simply not enough time or manpower for them to respond; you are on your own – better get a gun.

As I write this, a perfect example appeared on one of the news sites I monitor, appearing in The Western Journal, by Christine Favocci:

*NRA Study of Self-Defense Incidents

"It is often repeated by Second Amendment proponents because it is true: Bad guys with guns can only be stopped by good guys with guns. That is exactly what happened in a Chicago suburb yesterday when a home owner shot and killed an intruder after two men broke into his home and threatened him and his family at gunpoint.

According to the Arlington Heights Daily Herald, the unsuspecting family was at home in the afternoon when the two invaders rang the doorbell. When the homeowner opened the door the two perpetrators forced their way in, demanded money and threatened the family with guns. The mother and two children fled to an upstairs bedroom and locked the door. The homeowner managed to fight of one of the intruders who fled the scene, and then, while he retrieved his gun from the master bedroom, he was attacked by the remaining intruder. A vicious struggle ensued, resulting in the homeowner finally able to shoot and kill the intruder and save his family."

In most cases, being armed while outside the home is easier if you carry concealed. This, of course requires a concealed handgun license, issued by your local sheriff (more on this later).

In "open carry" states like Oregon and many other western states (except California), you may legally carry your loaded gun without needing a license. Remember though in some states, like Oregon, legislatures have given municipalities the authority to enact their own ordinances limiting open carry to only those who possess a current Concealed Handgun License.

This makes no sense, of course, but what should you expect from lawmakers who are ignorant about most things, especially guns.

Depending on the state you are in, an open carry gun must be obviously displayed to the extent that a law enforcement officer could readily identify such possession. Practically speaking, this means that while in your vehicle, the gun must be visible either on the passenger seat, or preferably on the dashboard and in a holster. While carried on your person and not in your vehicle, the gun should be in a holster and not shielded by clothing.

Carrying a gun while backpacking or camping in forest lands is perfectly legal as long as you are not in the city limits. Common sense would suggest that if nothing else, the threat from cougars or mountain lions would necessitate being armed.

As handgun laws vary among the states and are always subject to change, it is your responsibility to know the laws in whatever state you intend to carry a gun. My favorite resource for this information is the website handgunlaw.us, which explains in detail the handgun laws of every state.

What about the psychology of self-defense? Are you mentally prepared to do what might be necessary to defend yourself and your family? Would you be able to pull the trigger against a human attacker? You must be able to answer these questions. While it might be true that in many cases, the mere presence of a gun in your hand is enough to scare the assailant into running away, it is not a sure thing to rely on*.

Thugs are not rational people; they are often on drugs and do not care what they have to do to get more of them. If you are in their way, they may think nothing of killing you to get what they want. I asked an ex-friend of mine who lost his home in the 2008 recession and went to the dark side, why he became so self destructive by dealing drugs. His answer was "desperate times call for desperate measures."

Deadly Force
How do you decide at what point the use of deadly force becomes necessary? Fortunately, the laws do affirm your right of self-defense, notwithstanding gun hating judges. You get to determine if your life is being threatened, or if the lives of any innocent people in your immediate vicinity are being threatened, and you get to decide what level of response is necessary to <u>stop that threat</u>.

*NRA Study of Self-Defense Incidents

Your obligation is to be able to explain your decisions, such that a reasonable person would agree with your actions based on the circumstances of the incident.

The distance from you to the assailant is a critical factor in a life threatening situation, as is whether or not the assailant is armed. For example, if the armed assailant is within arms length from you, there is little doubt as to a proper response. If however, the potential assailant is 25 feet away and is not displaying a weapon, you not only have a little time, but you are obligated to properly assess the situation, answering such questions as, can the situation be defused without escalation? If the situation does develop into clearly life threatening, and you still have separation, drawing your gun and commanding the assailant to stop advancing, might be the next step.

If these warning measures do not effect an end of the threat, or if the assailant's advance is immediate and violent, and certainly if the assailant now displays a weapon of any kind, you may decide that there is no other option but to pull the trigger. Your objective is to stop the threat; once that is accomplished, you must stop shooting. For example, if the assailant drops his weapon and starts to run away after being shot, you cannot continue to shoot at him while he is running away.

While you do get to make these decisions based on your best judgment, this is a heavy responsibility with potential legal liability. The test of your decision to use deadly force is based on the "reasonable man" doctrine. That is, if a reasonable person would agree with your actions considering the circumstances of the incident, you would be within the laws of self-defense. This is my non-lawyer understanding of current State law, and is generally the understanding of the law enforcement community in most rural counties in the west. Unfortunately, in major cities like Portland and Seattle, there are gun-hating judges who apparently do not care what their State law says, and instead, impose their own bias' on victims who dare to try to defend themselves*.

Recently, there was a case in the south where a troubled man, but legally armed, was harassing a female sitting in her car in a parking space for the handicapped, but did not appear to be so. The husband, a large and imposing man, came out from the store, grabbed the harasser and threw him to the ground. On the video, the husband then turned away to clearly dis-engage from the contact, but the armed man, now sitting on the pavement, fired his weapon anyway into the back of the husband. There was some initial hesitation from law enforcement, but the shooter was eventually charged with murder.

* Case of Michael Stricland in Portland, Oregon

Choosing a Gun

Choosing your first gun can be a daunting task, given the abundance of choices while standing at the gun counter looking at 6 or 7 guns that all look the same, not to mention the never ending recommendations from friends. There are different manufacturers, models, calibers, and so on. There are revolvers and semi-automatics and there are different opinions on every one of them.

When I see a client who is in the market for their first gun, I ask him or her what the main purpose will be for this gun. Is it mainly for home defense, or will it be used for concealed carry? If it is for home defense, a larger capacity gun (more ammunition) might be preferred. If it is for concealed carry, you would generally want a smaller frame and lighter weight gun. So, using that as a starting point we can begin the process of elimination to find the gun that is suitable for the client.

I do not receive any free guns from manufacturers, nor do I get any sales commission from any of the fine gun stores I might refer clients to. My opinions and recommendations are therefore, without compromise or conflict of interest.

Which gun is best – revolver vs. semi-automatic, double action/single action, .380, 9mm, 40 caliber? What do these terms even mean? We will get to that soon, but in the meantime I will say that the 3 most important factors to consider are **comfort, dependability, and sufficient firepower.**

Comfort

Comfort is a subjective decision for you alone to make. Comfort considerations include not only the weight, grip and feel of the gun and trigger, but most importantly the felt recoil as you shoot. It does you no good to buy a high quality gun if you do not practice with it because you cannot handle the recoil. Recoil is a function of and affected by, not only the caliber*, but also by the bullet weight, amount of powder loading, weight of the gun, and even the type of grip. Generally, the lighter the gun, the greater the felt recoil will be with the same caliber ammunition.

*Caliber is the diameter of the bullet, expressed in either inches or millimeters, with consideration of the shape of the bullet.

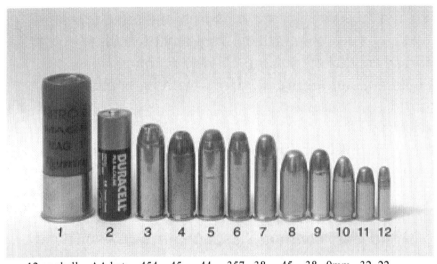

12 ga shell   AA bat   .454 .45   .44   .357 .38   .45   .38 9mm .32 .22

Dependability and Firepower - Revolvers

Dependability and firepower are fairly objective considerations. Even so, there is plenty of room for opinion. For example, many professionals would agree that a modern, double action revolver, because of its functional simplicity, is generally more reliable than a semi-automatic, especially in a stressful and immediate encounter, as you only have to point and shoot. Some would even stress that a hammerless or hidden hammer revolver is even more preferable since there is less chance of the gun getting snagged by a hammer as you draw your gun. For these reasons, a .38 special revolver is often recommended for first time gun owners

There are some drawbacks with revolvers however, which should be mentioned. One drawback is its lack of capacity – usually only 5 rounds. The double action trigger pull is usually longer and harder to pull than with single action. Accuracy might also be a consideration, in that a double action shot may not be as accurate for longer shots than would be with a cocked hammer. Also, There is significant recoil in calibers of .38 and above.

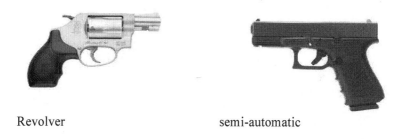

Revolver   semi-automatic

The point is, that if we are speaking about a novice shooter who does not practice much, a gun that you only have to point and shoot might be a good choice, especially considering that it would be used in a moment of high stress. Again the exception to this point may be the question of recoil sensitivity, which we will get to.

Double or single action refers to what happens to the hammer or striker when the trigger is pulled. In double action mode, pulling the trigger does two things, the hammer is both cocked and released, which is why the double action trigger pull is longer and requires more effort. With single action, as the hammer or striker is already cocked, pulling the trigger only causes the hammer to be released, which strikes the primer, which causes the powder to burn and expand, thus propelling the bullet down the barrel

As to firepower, the purpose of a self-defense weapon is to be able to stop a threat to your life as quickly as possible. Ideally, if we must shoot the assailant, we want that bullet (or those bullets) to have sufficient velocity and mass to cause enough damage to stop the attacker fast. It is not a question of killing the assailant, rather it is to stop the attack. One .22 bullet will kill a man eventually, but may not knock him down in his advance.

Many firearms professionals would argue that a self-defense handgun should be at least .40 caliber. Others would say 9mm or .380 would be the minimum for serious defensive purposes. For me, I say shot placement is more important than the bullet diameter. Five hits in the face with a .22 is much more effective than no hits with a .45.

At the range, gun safety is first.
Always assume that the gun is loaded until personally
verifying otherwise. Always handle the gun as if it were
loaded, and keep the gun pointed in a safe direction.
Always keep your finger off the trigger until ready to fire.
Always be sure of your backstop and what lies beyond.
Always clear your gun when you want to stop shooting as
there could be a round left in the chamber.

There is no substitute for actually shooting as many
different guns as might be on your list of potential guns
to purchase. Every gun is different in some way from
any other gun and those differences are revealed when
you shoot and compare. Many, many times a new client
will discover that their previous recommendations from
friends about a particular gun will be 100% wrong. For
example, a lady client will tell me that she has been told
that needs to get a .357 revolver, only to discover that she
barely has the finger strength to pull the trigger, and that
she has no tolerance for the recoil of a .357. Not only is
every gun different, but every shooter has different
strengths and limitations.

I normally start the process with a .22 semi-automatic and
a .22 revolver, shown below. This a comfortable way for
the client to start shooting with the almost non-existent
recoil of a .22, and is the most effective way to learn the
proper grip, stance and trigger control without

having to stress over the anticipated recoil of a larger caliber.

M&P compact 22

Ruger LCR 22

Ruger SR 22

After firing about 10 rounds each of the 22's, we move to try some .380 automatics. Sometimes, even the relatively light shooting .380's are too much for some clients and they decide on one of the .22's to be their gun.

Semi-Automatics
Usually, most will get used to the recoil of the .380 automatic and decide on this caliber. Some will even go on to the 9mm, but honestly, even though one can mitigate the recoil somewhat, by using "low recoil" ammunition, very few ladies will like and choose the .38 special revolver. Especially in a lightweight frame, as the recoil from a .38 can be very unpleasant.

Based on hundreds of clients, the favorite .380's for ladies are:

Sig Sauer P238

Springfield 911

Browning 1911/380

Walther CCP

Glock 42   M&P Shield 380

I had a gentleman client who also had very little tolerance for recoil, due to some medical issues, but wanted to purchase as powerful gun as possible for the purpose of home defense. He tried and liked the Kel Tec PMR 30, which had the capacity he wanted (30 rounds), and the power of the .22 Magnum round, but with very low recoil.

PMR 30

The question of recoil tolerance is most important in terms of practice. If one is thrust into a self-defense situation, his or her mind will not be on the "pain" of the recoil, but will be focused on survival and stopping the threat, and may even wish at that moment for more power.

However, if your gun is unpleasant for you to shoot because of felt recoil, you will likely not practice enough to get familiar and proficient with your gun, and then your chances of surviving a self-defense shooting would be diminished.

Often, a client will want the power of a 9mm but is not quite ready for the recoil. The use of a transition gun in .22 caliber might be helpful in a number of ways. First, the client can immediately get a gun that he or she can handle. Using the .22 for practice will help develop good shooting technique, and the continual practice will help overcome the aversion to recoil. When the shooter is ready, transitioning to that 9mm should be easily accomplished.

Modern semi-automatics can be sufficiently reliable to serve as your means of self-defense. As long as they are kept clean and lubricated, and you have maintained a skill level to be able to present your gun smoothly, quickly, and ready to fire, a good quality, semi-automatic is as reliable as any gun you might choose.

While revolvers rotate to feed the next round to the chamber, semi-automatics are fed by a spring-loaded magazine, which pushes the rounds up. When the trigger is pulled on a loaded semi-automatic, the top slide is pushed back from the force of the bullet, which automatically ejects the spent cartridge, cocks the hammer or striker, and then is returned to its original position by spring force, while at the same time pushing the next round into the firing chamber.

A modern, high quality semi-automatic pistol can be the right choice for you, depending your intended use. There are seemingly unlimited choices for finding the right one, ranging from .22 to .50 caliber, plastic frame or steel, double action, single action, or both, from compacts to the famous Desert Eagle.

Here are some of the most popular carry size guns in 9mm that my clients have chosen:

M&P Shield   Sig Sauer 365

Sig Sauer 320c   Springfield Hellcat

Glock 19

Glock 43 or 43X

Ruger Security 9

There are many options available for almost any gun that you end up with. If you want more capacity than your stock magazine, you can usually find magazine extensions adding two additional rounds.

Many manufacturers offer higher capacity magazines that will fit right into your gun. Lasers and high visibility sights are available for most guns. In low light conditions, a laser can be quite effective in speeding up your target acquisition. Some manufacturers are offering built in or factory attached lasers, as well as Red Dot optics on certain models.

Ammunition
Choosing the right ammunition for your gun, and for the purpose which it will be used, does not have to be complicated.

First, be sure you get the proper caliber, type, and pressure rating as noted in your owner's manual. For example, your gun may require a 9mm cartridge with normal pressure loading only. This means that no loads of higher pressure, such as +P or +P+ are to be used. These designations are always clearly printed on the box.

If your gun does allow for +P ammunition, you may use it, with an expectation of higher velocities and increased ballistic performance, but also with an expectation of a reduced life of the gun.

Bullet weight and type is also included in the description on the box. For example, you may see a description such as "9mm Nato, 115 grain MC." This means that the bullet is a full metal case, and weighs 115 grains.

Incidentally, 9mm, 9mm Nato, 9mm luger, 9x19, and 9mm Parabellum all refer to the same cartridge.

Another type of bullet is the Jacketed Hollow Point or JHP. This is usually the type of ammunition that is recommended for personal protection and self-defense, due to its combination of jacketing around the bullet for penetration into the target, and hollow point for expansion after penetration. For a 9mm pistol, you would see on the box a description such as 9mm Luger, 124 grain JHP.

"Low Recoil" ammunition like the <u>Federal Hydra-Shok</u> and <u>Hornady Critical Defense</u> is available for most calibers. This ammunition gets its properties from a combination of lower bullet weights and lower pressure loadings in the powder, and is somewhat effective at reducing felt recoil, but with a slight reduction in ballistics.

When you buy your first gun, know what your caliber feels like when shot. Figure out what your main use of the gun will be. Look for a good deal, but always choose quality over price when deciding on a tool to protect your life.

Defending Your Home

As I stated earlier, defending your home is first and foremost on the minds of most people these days. First, you will want do the obvious things to harden your perimeter:

1. Do not leave any keys outside or in your car.
2. Do not leave any doors or windows open at night.
3. Place outdoor lighting in dark areas where an invader could hide.
4. Install deadbolt locks, which cannot be defeated by "bumping."
5. Consider installing a security/alarm system, which can alert you if it detects a breach.

Whole books have been written on this subject alone, but you can add to this list any number of steps you might take to increase your odds of avoiding a random invasion.

Inside your home, you can place an inexpensive plug-in nightlight in areas where you would want increased visibility for you, in the event of having to confront intruders. You can get in the habit of locking your bedroom door while sleeping, so as to provide one last warning before an intruder might try to enter or break open the door, unless of course, there are young children in the house, in which case you would probably not want to have your door locked.

A Gun in the house
No doubt, you have heard all of the warnings about having a gun in the house, extolling the dangers to you and that it should be locked up and unloaded, or it should be in a big heavy safe, or that "statistics" show that you are more likely to shoot a family member than to prevail in a self-defense encounter.

All of this would be true if you were so irresponsible that you did not get competent training on gun safety and how to operate your gun properly and proficiently, if you did not practice shooting at the range, and at home in retrieving your gun, and if you were to leave loaded guns lying around where children might have access to them.

First, get a good quality portable safe with a quick access opening to put on your nightstand. The gun will be sufficiently locked up to prevent any curious hands from gaining access, but it will also be available for you to use, if necessary to defend your family! It makes no sense to have your only gun unloaded and in a place where you cannot quickly retrieve it.

All family members should participate in periodic discussions on what to do if there is an "emergency" in the house.

You can designate a "safe room" where all are to go to, and you can harden that room to whatever extent you wish, and can supply it with an extra cell phone, first aid kit, food and water, etc. **Be sure to take your gun with you into your safe room.**
If you are in your safe room while the invaders are elsewhere in the house, call the police for help. In describing the situation to the police, be sure to tell them what room you are in. Before you open the door, verify with the dispatcher that the police are definitely in the house and it is clear to open the door.

If your safe room idea does not work out for whatever reason, and you find yourself having to confront the intruders with your gun, remember it is they who have put your family's lives in danger.

Make your gun ready to fire, as you will likely not have time to do so upon confrontation. The mere fact that they are in your house means that your lives are threatened and that you therefore have the right to do whatever is necessary to stop that threat.

Do not assume that there is only one intruder just because you do not see others. After dealing with one, you must then verify that the house is clear. It is quite likely that any others have run away at the sound of gunfire, but you still must check. When the police do arrive, they should also do a room-by-room check. Make sure that you do not have a gun in your hand when the police arrive; better to have it in a holster at that point.

Realize, that after any incident involving gunfire, the police will, by policy, take possession of your firearm. The purpose of this policy is to hold any items of evidence that may be necessary in any potential future legal proceedings. They must return your property as soon as it is determined that no such proceedings are forthcoming, but this could be weeks or months.

It might be a good idea, and certainly is a good excuse, to own another gun for this eventuality.

Concealed Carry

"The right of the people to keep and bear arms shall not be infringed."

Is this not clearly written? It seems so to me, but let me put it another way:

The right of the people to own and carry firearms shall not be taken away or interfered with by government.

If these words mean what they say, then how can any state say that it is unlawful to carry a gun openly displayed, while at the same time effectively denying the people the ability to carry concealed, by way of draconian restrictions, fees, licensing, and arbitrary denials of concealed licenses by the Sheriff? If you cannot carry openly, and are effectively denied concealed carry, is this not infringement?

The best source of up to date information about handgun laws in all 50 states is the website handgunlaw.us. Here you will find not only all the handgun laws of your state, but also which other states recognize your license for purposes of carrying concealed in that state.

Oregon   Shall Issue   **Must Inform O**
(See Must Inf

Honors OR Permit
OR Permit Not Honored
OR Res Permits Only

Note: Alaska, Arizona, Arkansas, Kansas, Kentucky, Maine, Mississippi, Missouri, New Hampshire, Oklahoma, South Dakota, Vermont and West Virginia have "Permitless Carry." Anyone who can legally possess a firearm may carry it concealed in these states without a Permit/License. Check each states page for more information and any restrictions that may apply.

Idaho, North Dakota and Wyoming
have "**Permitless Carry**" for their Residents only.

Permits/Licenses This State Honors Listed Below

Oregon does not honor any other state Permit/Licenses.

Take for example the previous page, showing in light grey, the 22 states that recognize the Oregon license.

Many license holders also get the Arizona permit, which you can do entirely by mail directly with their Concealed carry division:

Arizona

Note: Alaska, Arizona, Arkansas, Kansas, Kentucky, Maine, Mississippi, Missouri, New Hampshire, Oklahoma, South Dakota, Vermont and West Virginia have "Permitless Carry." Anyone who can legally possess a firearm may carry it concealed in these states without a Permit/License. Check each states page for more information and any restrictions that may apply.

Idaho, North Dakota and Wyoming
have "Permitless Carry" for their Residents only.

Permits/Licenses This State Honors Listed Below

With both the Oregon License and the Arizona license you will have a total of 32 states that recognize one or both of your licenses and certainly opens the country for easier travel.

Most western states now have "Shall Issue" laws, which means that the local sheriff cannot deny a license to any legal adult for arbitrary reasons. All states have their own laws regarding the carrying of concealed handguns. There are many minor differences among the states, mostly as to where you cannot carry even with a license. For example, Utah says you cannot carry in a church. In other words, a criminal or lunatic, who would not care what the law is anyway, may be carrying, but law-abiding citizens are prohibited from being able to defend themselves. Gun free zones mean that while the criminal may be armed, you are not.

Many states have restrictions on carrying in a school zone or on school property. However, these laws do not seem to be very effective in preventing those deranged soles from murdering their classmates or killing a bunch of innocent children if they are determined to do so.

Some states, have no such restrictions on their citizens. For example, currently in Oregon, there are only four restrictions on where you can carry a concealed gun, and no government entity, other than the State Legislature, may add or increase any restriction on your rights.

These restriction are:

1. Courthouses
2. Federal Buildings
3. Secure parts of the Airports
4. Privately owned businesses that have a "no firearms" policy, but only if they have informed you of that policy.

Courthouses will have clear signage and metal detectors at the entry point, but inferior court facilities, like the district attorney's offices or the grand jury facilities, may only have signage to advise you of the penalties for possessing a gun in those areas.

Federal buildings include, but are not limited to IRS, Social Security, Post Offices, HHS and so on. At the TSA security point at the airport it is very clear that you should not attempt to pass with any part of gun in your possession. I once had an empty magazine in my carry-on bag that I had forgotten about. The magazine was confiscated, but not until I was berated and threatened by the pleasant TSA agent.

While government bureaucrats at any level have no right to create policies contrary to state law, privately owned businesses have the absolute right to establish their own policies regarding firearms on their own property.

If they wish to enforce this policy however, they must sufficiently inform you of its existence. Of the misguided business owners who have a "no firearms" policy, most simply put up a sign in the entry to accomplish this notification. However, if you do not see the sign, and you have not been otherwise notified, it would seem logical that this policy would not apply to you, and you could therefore legally maintain the ability to defend yourself by holding on to your concealed guns.

In Aurora Colorado a few years ago, movie goers were subjected to a massacre by a lone crazed gunman, who apparently, was the only person in the theatre with a gun. There were seven theatres in the area all showing the same movie, but this theatre was the only one that had a "no firearms" policy. Did the gunman choose this theatre for that reason?

A couple of years ago my sister and I were in Tucson where we stopped at an apparently popular coffee shop for breakfast. After ordering, I looked around this packed restaurant and noticed that every single table and booth was occupied by men and women wearing their guns on there hips. I never felt so safe while in a public place!

The politicians do not know what to do about mass murderers, and most of them are also ignorant about guns. Their solutions usually involve some attack on law abiding gun owners by way of new restrictions on gun cosmetics, magazines, locking requirements, etc. None of these things, in the hands of law abiding gun owners, will ever murder someone, but in the politicians minds, they are at least "doing something."

Recently, there is a big move to enact "red light" laws. Admittedly, there could be some merit in encouraging people who have some substantiated knowledge of another person's apparent intention to carry out a mass murder, to come forth to inform the authorities of this potential threat. As usual though, the politicians and the gun hating lobby have screwed up what could have been a useful tool in prevention. Instead of providing the ability for law enforcement to interview the subject and gather and verify more evidence and before due process of law would take hold, they instead, defy our Constitution and allow confiscation of the subject's firearms based on sometimes mere accusations from strangers or on the the flimsiest of evidence!

Carrying

How you choose to carry your gun is a personal decision that only you can make. The size of the gun will tend to dictate the most comfortable way for you, but in any case your chosen method must provide not only comfort, but a secure retention of the gun. Many people, including celebrities like Plaxico Burris of the New York Giants, have faced prison time for negligence when their gun has fallen and accidentally discharged.

Gun professionals will tell you that even if you just stick your gun in a pants pocket, you should have a means of securing it, such as a pocket holster. Holsters are designed to cover of the trigger to reduce the chance of accidental discharge and are shaped to provide a degree of retention.

There are so many choices for holsters that many of us sometimes find that they have boxes full of them that were bought for a certain gun, or style of wearing that they no longer use. I still have an old shoulder holster for when I had dreams of being James Bond, or an old ankle holster that made me walk funny.

Holsters are usually made for a certain model of gun. They can be made for hip carry on the inside or outside the pants, for cross draw in the front, or for the small of the back.

These holsters are designed to be worn with a <u>gun</u> belt, which is thicker, wider, and stiffer than a dress belt.

Other forms of carry include purses that have a proper holster inside, gun cases disguised as phone case or briefcase, elastic belly bands, and fanny packs with a built in holster and quick opening zippers. These fanny packs are particularly handy when hiking.

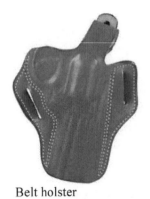

Belt holster

Purse Holster

Fanny Pack

Holster shorts

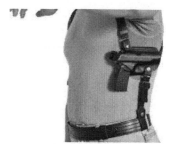

Pocket Holster   Shoulder Holster

Gun Safety

When you are carrying, no matter which method you
have chosen, always know the "condition" of your gun.
Condition in this case, means whether or not your gun is
ready to fire. If you have a loaded revolver, it is in
condition one (ready to fire). If you have a loaded semi-
automatic with the trigger in double action mode, you are
in condition one and ready to fire. However, if you have
a semi-automatic with a full magazine, but do not have a
round loaded in the chamber, you must know that to
make your gun ready to fire, it will require a full
retraction and release of the slide.

When I practice with my carry gun, I always include
racking the slide in my drills. My initial action is to draw
the gun, rack the slide, and hold in the "low ready
position" until bringing up to fire. Practicing the low
ready position provides some muscle memory for what I
prefer and might expect in an actual situation.

Low ready Position

The purpose of the low ready position is to be ready, but to not yet present the gun until fire is required. Additionally, in a situation that does not require immediate fire, you should keep your finger off the trigger to prevent an unintentional discharge. Always re-confirm your gun's condition before re-holstering.

When you are carrying concealed outside the home, you are required to possess your Concealed Handgun License in the same way you are required to possess your driver's license when operating a motor vehicle.

Interactions with Law Enforcement
If you are stopped by the police for a traffic violation, it may be unpleasant, but it is not something to be overly stressed about, as long as you remember a few simple things.

First, leave your gun wherever it is and do not touch it again until the stop is concluded. Then, before the officer gets up to your window, retrieve your wallet and papers, so that when he does present himself, the only things he sees are your hands containing your papers. If you are carrying openly, advise him so, but do not point or move toward it.

If you are carrying concealed, simply hand him your driver's license, registration, insurance card and your concealed handgun license while letting him know that you are carrying. Even though you are not required by law to inform him, it is a courtesy that I would certainly want if I were on the other end. When he runs your drivers license, the dispatcher will confirm to him that you hold a valid concealed handgun license.

There is no truth to the rumor that offering him a nice fresh donut will help you in any way.

Practice
If you rarely practice your shooting for accuracy, speed, and technique, you have little hope against an armed assailant, even at a distance of only 15 feet.

Reacting under the pressure of a life and death encounter will affect the shooting ability of almost anyone, except perhaps, John Wayne, who said something like:

"Son, it's not enough to be just a good shot, you also have to be willing."

Being willing, means that you are willing to take the risk of exposing your body sufficiently to make the shot. When the shooting starts, the natural reaction is to hit the deck and take cover. Only the willing will stand and shoot.

Practicing to prepare for a self-defense situation involves much more than going to the range to shoot a box of ammunition under controlled conditions at 20 feet. What if the assailant is 2 feet away, as is the case in most of the self-defense shootings studied by the NRA? What about drawing your gun smoothly and quickly in a moment of high stress. What if the assailant is wearing body armor, and your only chance is a head shot?

A good practice session will include both target shooting for accuracy, using the sights on your gun to properly aim, as well as combat, or point shooting, where both eyes are focused on the target instead of the front sight. In a real life confrontation where the armed assailant is only a few feet away, you will likely not have time to line up your sights.

Rather, pointing your gun and shooting quickly with your focus on the attacker will be an automatic response; shouldn't you therefore, practice for it?

Your range or club may not allow drawing and shooting, but you can find a safe place to shoot, out of the city limits, that has a suitable backstop in order to practice. Or, you can easily practice drawing, racking and pointing at home. Just be absolutely sure that your gun is unloaded before doing this exercise.

Drawing Your Gun
At what point is it legal to draw and present your gun? The law says that if there is a direct and credible threat to your life, or the lives of any innocent people in your immediate vicinity, you have the right to take whatever action is necessary and reasonable to stop that threat.

So, if you draw your gun for the purpose of responding to that direct and credible threat, you should be within your legal rights. If however, there is not yet a credible threat against you, but draw your gun for the purpose of intimidating just a potential threat, you could be cited for brandishing a firearm or menacing with a firearm. Be sure of your situation before taking these precarious steps.

What about pulling the trigger? For me, that will done as a last resort – when I have concluded, maybe in a split second, that this is the only way I can save my life. If I do pull the trigger, it better be because the assailant has a weapon in his hand, otherwise the obvious question will be, why did you have to shoot him?

If you are involved in a self-defense shooting and the assailant is down on the ground with bullet wounds, hopefully you have survived relatively unharmed. What follows though, will not be much fun.

You cannot assume that the assailant is dead, or that he is not able to use a weapon on you, so you must not get near him, and you must be ready to continue the fight if necessary. Obviously, you must contact 911 to report the situation and to request assistance and perhaps an ambulance. Keep this conversation simple and straightforward in a way that conveys only the situation at hand, as this will be recorded. You could say something like: "Hello 911, I am the victim of an attack, my life was threatened and I had to defend myself, the attacker is down, please send help." When the patrolman arrives, holster your gun or place it on the floor or ground and identify yourself to him.

After he verifies that that you are the victim, he will ask you to explain what happened. Now, many lawyers will tell you not to say anything at this point.

However, there is a body lying on the ground, and unless you want to immediately go jail, you should at least briefly describe the circumstances to the officer while emphasizing the fact that your life was threatened. You will at some point have to provide a full statement, at which time you may wish to have your lawyer present.

There are plans and organizations that provide for assistance if you should find yourself charged with a crime stemming from a self-defense shooting. These plans go beyond plain liability insurance by specifying that the assistance provided will be for defending you against such charges. The "Armed Citizens Defense Network" is one of the best plans to check out. For a little over $100 per year, they will send a gun lawyer to you and provide up to a $10,000 retainer to initiate a defense on your behalf, if you are in this situation.

Some Discussion Questions

Q. When outside your home, under what circumstances can you rightfully draw your gun?

A. When faced with a direct and credible threat to your life, you would be within your rights to draw your weapon.

Q. Does an assailant have to have a weapon in his hand before you can shoot him?

A. Not necessarily, as the law does not include this as a requirement for legal self-defense. If the circumstances are such that the defender would have had a reasonable expectation of death, or at least great bodily harm at the hands of the assailant, he would likely be within the law to shoot.

Q. What is the first thing to say to the 911 dispatcher, when reporting being attacked?

A. "I am the victim."

Q. Can you act as a deputy sheriff because you have a Concealed Handgun License?

A. No. the CHL only proves that you have been cleared by the Sheriff as a legal adult and are authorized to carry concealed.

Q. Should you fire a warning shot while inside the city limits.

A. It is illegal to discharge a firearm inside the city limits, unless it is part of an act of self-defense. The danger of firing a warning shot is the possibility of injuring a bystander or neighbor.

Q. If you possess a Concealed Handgun License, can you carry in national parks.

A. Yes. The holder of a valid license may carry in any national park in the state in which the license was issued.

Cases for Study

The 2am reality check

Back in younger days, I was at home in bed at 2am when I heard a noise that awakened me. I opened my eyes in disbelief to see a scruffy looking punk opening my door and entering my bedroom. Apparently he had gained access through a barely locked back door and had grabbed my watch and a small amount of cash on his way up the stairs.

I always have and always will have a gun by my bed (a habit from Vietnam no doubt), so I grabbed my pistol and racked the slide. Hearing that noise, he turned and bolted down the stairs and out the door. As I said, I was younger then, so in anger, I chased after him not exactly sure what I would do next.

He managed to disappear into the night, but at this point I realized that I was standing in the middle of the street, almost naked, with a gun in my hand. Time to go inside and think about tomorrow when I will put better locks on the doors.

Robbery in the Diner

Joe and Carol were sitting in the diner having lunch. Joe, who had a Concealed Handgun License, always carried his pistol when out of the house.

All of a sudden Joe noticed a young teenager walking into the diner and approaching the cashier with what looked like a gun in his hand. Obviously, the teenager was attempting to rob the cashier.

A million thoughts raced through Joe's mind. Should he intervene? Should he confront the robber? If so, would there then be shooting caused by just the act of confrontation?

If the cashier's life is in danger should he just shoot the robber to save her life? What if he did shoot, but missed the robber and accidentally shot a waitress? Or, what if he did manage to shoot the robber, and it turned out later that he was only 14, the gun was not real, and the teenager is now paralyzed for life?

Absent any shots being fired by the robber, or any direct threat to Joe, the best course of action might be to do nothing, except to be ready. The robber would, more than likely, just run away with the money and no lives would be lost.

Road Rage

I was on my way to the store when I stopped at the intersection to let the vehicle on the right proceed. As I turned left to follow him down the road, he all of a sudden slowed to a crawl. Since it was a 35mph zone, I innocently passed him and then returned to the right lane in front of him.

For some reason this guy freaked out. He was riding my rear bumper, honking, and shaking his fist.

Thinking that if I turn off the road, he might lose interest in being a lunatic, I turned to the right and stopped at the side of the road. He turned after me, went to the corner and then turned back to pull up next to me headed in the opposite direction.

Considering his behavior, but not knowing his intentions, I had my gun in hand and loaded a round, but did not present the gun. He had something in his hand and was manipulating it somewhat, while I was trying to see what it was. As it turned out, it was his cell phone and for unknown purposes, he was taking my picture.

Then, as he drove away, I was thinking that it was a good thing I did not present my gun, for it to be in that picture.

Coming Home

Rocky and Lucy decided to go out to dinner. Rocky, being a conscientious gun owner and concealed license holder, decided to carry his smaller and more comfortable pistol tonight, rather than his regular Sig Sauer 226.

There had been some trouble downtown where the restaurant was located, so Lucy, who also had a license, volunteered to carry the Sig in her purse, just in case. The Sig 226 is a double/single, which means that you can load a round and then de-cock the hammer, putting the gun in a loaded but safe double action mode.

Anyway, after a pleasant dinner they drove home, and as they got out of the car, Rocky had a strange sense that something wasn't quite right. Hiding in the bushes near the front door were two armed thugs, one with a knife and one with a hatchet, who started coming for Rocky. Rocky pulled his gun and aimed for the first attacker, but his gun jammed. By that time, Lucy had the Sig in hand and quickly and permanently did away with the two sorry souls.

Don't mess with Lucy!

The Dark Parking Lot

Betsy was working late at her office one night. Finally
the day's work was done, and she prepared to leave.

It was fall, and the days were getting shorter and darkness
came rather quickly. Earlier, in the morning when she
had arrived, the only space available was toward the edge
of the parking lot near the trees. Parking under or near
one of the lights would been preferable, but today, she
did not have that option.

As she left the building and started walking toward her
car, she fully realized that she was quite alone and rather
vulnerable. She decided to put her keys in her left hand,
and place her right hand on her .38 special revolver,
which was in in a holster in her purse, which was carried
over her shoulder with a reinforced leather strap.

As she got near her car, a rather scruffy and deranged
looking man appeared about 20 feet in front of her. She
loudly commanded him to stay where he was and to not
come any closer. If he obeyed her command, perhaps she
could avoid an unpleasant confrontation.

He did not obey her command, and started to move
toward her. Because of the fact that he ignored her

first command, she concluded that her life was now in danger, and drew her gun. She loudly commanded "I said, stop where you are; I do not want to shoot you, but I most assuredly will if you don't stop!"

Upon seeing the gun, and realizing his situation, the assailant fled through the trees.

Betsy got into her car, locked the doors, and made her exit. She then called 911 to report the incident, in the hopes that some attention might be directed toward better securing that parking lot.

The Failed Church Massacre

Scott worked in one of the major sporting goods stores in Medford, Oregon. As an avid fisherman, hunter, and self-defense expert, he always kept his skills honed to the highest level. His favorite personal weapon was the Springfield EMP-4, and he practiced with that gun until he could hit a nickel at 30 feet.

Scott was also a religious man, and attended his church every Sunday. As there are no restrictions on carrying a gun in church in Oregon, Scott was always armed, willing to protect his fellow parishioners at whatever cost to himself.

Then it happened. One Sunday a lone lunatic came rushing into the church service, spraying bullets everywhere with his AR-15. Scott happened to be slightly behind and to the side of the crazed gunman, and with a quick aim, put two rounds in the back of the head of the man destined for hell.

Scott's quick and deadly action put and end to what could have been another massacre. No innocent lives were lost that day.

Appendix

Interesting Self Defense Findings
From reports to NRA's "Armed Citizen"
(482 incidents over a 5 year period)

The shooting distance in the vast majority of cases was slightly in excess of arm's length.

The majority of incidents (52%) took place in the home, followed by the workplace (32%), while 7% occurred around vehicles.

The most common initial crimes were armed robbery (32%), home invasion (30%), and burglary (18%).

The average number of shots fired by the victim against the perpetrator was 2.

Handguns were used by the defender in 78% of the incidents; rifles or shotguns in the balance.

The most common calibers were the 9mm, .38, and .357; 23% of the handguns used were .380 caliber or less.

The firearm was carried on the body of the defender in only 20% of the incidents; 80% were retrieved from a place of storage.

Single assailants were involved in 64% of the cases, with multiple conspirators being in 36%. However, when the shooting starts, immediate flight is the most common response by assailants, and/or lookouts at the sound of gunfire.

With few exceptions, criminals ceased their advances immediately upon being shot. Even .380 "mouse guns" displayed a significant degree of lethality when employed at close range.

Additional Resources

There is no end to information available to you about being armed, proper shooting technique, and specifics about your particular gun.

YouTube
I dare say, thousands of videos can be found here, covering every aspect of shooting.

Internet
Type in your gun manufacturer and model and you will be offered many reviews of your gun by leading experts. Ammoland.com, and Guns.com, are two good websites to check out.

Radio
Gun Talk, A weekly radio program hosted by Tom Gresham.

Magazines
Such magazines as Guns & Ammo, Handguns, Shooting, Concealed Carry, etc. always include informative articles covering all of the subjects in this book.

Books
Hundreds, if not thousands of books have been written about guns and shooting. A few to consider are:

The Basics of Pistol Shooting, National Rifle Association

Effective Defense-The Woman, The Plan, The Gun, by Gila May Hayes

Deadly Force, by Massad Ayoob

NRA Guide to the Basics of Personal Protection Outside the Home, National Rifle Association

Understanding Oregon Gun Laws, by Kevin Starrett of the Oregon Firearms Federation

Oregon Concealed, by Don Leach

In addition to your own practice sessions where you maintain your shooting skills, there are professionally managed upscale courses, such as *Thunder Ranch, Front Sight,* and others.

A training course that I found most effective is *Virtual Safe Shot*, located in Fair Oaks, California. By using actual pistols, not loaded, but attached to the computer to give realistic feel, and instant feedback on your shooting effectiveness, you can accomplish in a couple of hours, what would take you days at the range.

Useful Shooting Drills

The Draw
Practice drawing your gun to a low ready position, and then to a shooting position. This can be done at home with an unloaded gun, or at a range (if allowed) using your loaded gun. Start slowly, and be careful not to have your finger on the trigger until the gun is positioned to fire.

Failure to Stop
To simulate an initial failure to stop an attacker, from a low ready position, bring the gun up and fire two shots at center mass, then one shot to the head.

Reloading
Shoot five rounds only, then reload and shoot five more.

Malfunctions
To simulate misfires in a revolver, and to assess your trigger control, skip a round in the cylinder and fire until empty. In semi-auto's add one or two dummy rounds in the live full magazine, and then shoot. You will practice recognition and reaction procedures.

Low Light
The best way to practice low light conditions is indoors, with the lights turned off, and using an unloaded, laser equipped gun to assess your ability to quickly put the gun on target.

Shooting from Cover
Practice shooting from behind a simulated barricade.

Combination
Combine these drills in various stages, and practice shooting with only one hand.